WHY CHEMISTRY MATTER

NON-METALS

Adrienne
Montgomerie

Crabtree Publishing Company

www.crabtreebooks.com

Crabtree Publishing Company

www.crabtreebooks.com

Author: Adrienne Montogomerie
Publishing plan research and development:
  Sean Charlebois, Reagan Miller
  Crabtree Publishing Company
Project Editor: Tom Jackson
Editor: Adrianna Morganelli
Proofreader: Wendy Scavuzzo
Project Coordinator: Kathy Middleton
Designer: Karen Perry
Cover Design: Demetra Peppas
Picture Researcher: Sophie Mortimer
Managing Editor: Tim Harris
Art Director: Jeni Child
Editorial Director: Lindsey Lowe
Children's Publisher: Anne O'Daly
Production and Print Coordinator: Katherine Berti
Prepress Technician: Katherine Berti

Photographs:
Cover: Shutterstock: Joe Belanger
Interior: Alchemist-HP: 27t; **Robert Hunt Library:** 11b; **Science Photo Library:** Charles D. Winters 18; **Shutterstock:** 10, 19, 21t, B. Alin 12, Nikola Bilic 26, V. Blinov 5t, Coprid 25, Vit Kovalcik 17b, Stephen McSweeny 13, Picsfive 21b, Anatoliy Samara 9t, Alistair Scott 27b, Emran Mohd Tamil 14, Margaret I. Wallace 16, Ji Zhou 22; **Thinkstock:** Goodshoot 23, Hemera 24, 28, iStockphoto 9b, 17t, Photos.com 4, 5b, 6, 7, 8, 11t, 20, 29.

All artwork and diagrams © Brown Bear Books Ltd.

Produced for Crabtree Publishing Company
by Brown Bear Books Ltd.

Library and Archives Canada Cataloguing in Publication

Montgomerie, Adrienne
    Metals / Adrienne Montgomerie.

(Why chemistry matters)
Includes index.
Issued also in electronic format.
ISBN 978-0-7787-4231-9 (bound).--ISBN 978-0-7787-4235-7 (pbk.)

    1. Metals--Juvenile literature. I. Title. II. Series: Why chemistry matters

QD171.M66 2012   j546'.3   C2012-906391-6

Library of Congress Cataloging-in-Publication Data

CIP available at Library of Congress

Crabtree Publishing Company

www.crabtreebooks.com 1-800-387-7650

Printed in the U.S.A./112012/FA20121012

Published in Canada
Crabtree Publishing
616 Welland Ave.
St. Catharines, ON
L2M 5V6

Published in the United States
Crabtree Publishing
PMB 59051
350 Fifth Avenue, 59th Floor
New York, New York 10118

Published in the United Kingdom
Crabtree Publishing
Maritime House
Basin Road North, Hove
BN41 1WR

Published in Australia
Crabtree Publishing
3 Charles Street
Coburg North
VIC, 3058

Contents

What Is a Non-metal?

What makes an **element** a **non-metal**? When it is not a **metal**. Non-metal elements are varied, but they do share a few common properties.

Elements are either metal, non-metal, or **metalloid**. There are 118 elements in all and most of those are metals. Only 19 are classified as non-metals.

The **compounds** of non-metal elements make up most of the body of a living thing and most of Earth's landscape—the rocks, oceans, and air. Pure, non-metal elements can be either **solids** or **gases** (just one is a **liquid**). The solid elements tend to be crumbly crystals. They do not **conduct** heat or electricity very well, so that makes them good **insulators**.

Carbon is the most common solid non-metal. It is the material in charcoal.

The non-metal selenium is found in Brazil nuts. We need tiny amounts of this element in our food to be healthy.

Insulators are materials that do not let energy move through them. They block electric currents and that makes them useful for shielding people from electric shocks. Insulators also stop heat from spreading through them. That means they will keep cold things cold and hot things hot.

Non-metals are not magnetic. They cannot produce a magnetic field, and a magnet will not attract or stick to them. Non-metal elements also combine to form **acids**. Acids are compounds that react with alkalies, which form from metals.

Metal or Non-metal?

Divide a piece of paper in half to make a chart. Label one side "Metal," and the other side "Non-metal." Arrange the list of properties below on your chart. Which side does each one go on —metal or non-metal? (Some of them might go on both sides.)

- *conducts electricity*
- *magnetic*
- *breaks easily when bent*
- *shiny when polished*
- *can be pulled into a wire*
- *crumbly crystals*
- *can be hammered flat*
- *melts at a very high temperature*
  - *squishy*
    - *insulator*
      - *glows when hot*
        - *dissolves in water*
          - *rusts or tarnishes*

Atomic Structure

Everything is made of **atoms**. Atoms are the smallest units of an element. The structure of their atom is what makes non-metals different from other elements.

Every atom of one element has the same structure. Changing the structure will change the element to which that atom belongs. Every atom is made of **electrons** circling a nucleus that contains **protons** and **neutrons**.

The electrons move in an area called an **electron shell**. Each shell can contain a maximum number of electrons—most hold eight. Atoms with a lot of electrons have a lot of shells. In general, all the electron shells in an atom are full, except the outer one. The electrons in the outer shell are the parts of the atom that get involved in chemical **reactions**. The number of outer electrons controls how the atoms react and form bonds with other atoms. Most non-metal elements have atoms with nearly full outer electron shells.

A match head has sulfur atoms, and the box side contains phosphorus. When the two non-metals are pushed together, they react and create a flame.

A space shuttle's engines were powered by two non-metals—hydrogen and oxygen.

Atoms become involved in reactions and bond together so they can make a full outer shell and become stable. Metal atoms have one or two outer electrons, and the atoms become stable by dropping their outer electrons. Non-metals do the opposite—they pick up extra electrons to fill the empty spaces in the outer shell.

Electrons have a negative **charge**. Losing electrons transforms an atom into a positive **ion**. Adding electrons turns an atom into a negative ion. Opposites attract in chemistry, so a positive (metal) ion bonds to a negative (non-metal) ion. Non-metal atoms can also bond in another way. Two or more atoms can move together so their outer shells touch, then share their outer electrons so the atoms all become stable.

Non-metal Electrons

The outer electron shell of non-metals ranges from half full (carbon) to completely full (neon). A non-metal atom can bond to other non-metal atoms by sharing electrons so their outer shells are filled. It can also collect electrons dropped by metal atoms. Non-metals such as neon do not form bonds. Their outer shell is already full.

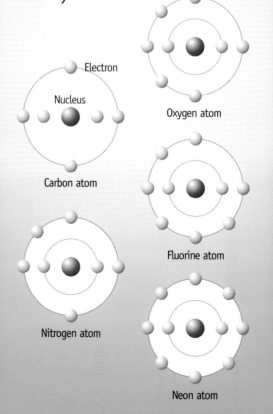

Electron

Nucleus

Oxygen atom

Carbon atom

Fluorine atom

Nitrogen atom

Neon atom

The Halogens

Group 7 of the periodic table contains the non-metal elements called the halogens. They are highly reactive and have many different uses from cleaning products to fireproofing.

The halogens are fluorine, chlorine, bromine, iodine, and astatine. Fluorine and chlorine are gases. Iodine and astatine are solids. In normal conditions, bromine is a liquid. It is the only liquid non-metal, and one of just two liquid elements (mercury is the other).

Halogens are some of the most reactive non-metal elements. This feature is due to their atomic structure. Halogen atoms have seven out of eight electrons in their outer shells. Just one more would make them stable. As a result, halogens have a powerful pull on the outer electrons of other atoms, and often **react** with them.

Chlorine is used to keep swimming pools clean.

Halogen bulbs are very bright. Halogen gas inside the bulb prevents the metal filament from breaking.

Fluoride Toothpaste

Most toothpastes contain fluoride. This is a chemical containing the halogen fluorine. The fluoride coats your teeth to prevent chemicals in food from reacting with the calcium in tooth enamel and making it thin and weak. Fluorine is more reactive than calcium, so it always reacts first.

Few other non-metal atoms can pull as strongly as halogen atoms. Halogens form compounds with metal and non-metal elements.

Fluorine is the most reactive non-metal element of all. It will even react with glass, so it has to be kept in thick metal containers. However, when fluorine bonds with other elements the compounds are very stable. For example, fluorine bonds with carbon and hydrogen to form Teflon, the slippery substance used in nonstick pans.

The next most reactive halogen is chlorine. (Bromine and iodine are even less reactive. Very rare astatine is the least reactive of all.) Sodium hypochlorite is a chlorine compound used in bleach. Bleach reacts with colored chemicals—just about anything—and turns them white. It is used to whiten clothing and paper, and also as a powerful cleaner.

The halogens react with anything, even the chemicals in living things. This makes them poisonous, so they are used as pesticides and disinfectants. Powerful chlorine compounds are in cleaners, while weaker iodine compounds are used to clean the germs from cuts while still being gentle on the skin.

Small amounts of chlorine and iodine are important elements for staying healthy. Iodine is needed to make a hormone (chemical messenger) called thyroxine. This substance is the gas pedal of the body. It controls how fast the body's systems run.

Dead Sea

In the Middle East, between Israel and Jordan, there is a lake named the Dead Sea. It contains some of the world's saltiest water. Not many animals can survive there, which is why we know it as "dead." The salt is made from halogen compounds, mainly of bromine and chlorine. They are washed out of rocks into the water. The salt increases the density of the water, which means objects float higher in salt water. There is so much salt dissolved in the Dead Sea that humans can easily float in the water.

Halogens are found in many cleaning products.

Chlorine ions (known as chloride) have many uses in body chemistry.

We get chlorine from the most familiar halogen compound, something you use every day. You probably put it on your food, and you may use it to melt ice on sidewalks. Sodium chloride—table salt—is found in rocks and in the oceans.

Sodium chloride is formed by combining one atom of sodium with one atom of chlorine. Sodium is a very reactive metal with one outer electron. It gives this to the chlorine to form a positive sodium ion and a negative chlorine ion. These two ions bond to form a salt **molecule**.

Chemical Weapon

In World War I (1914–1918), chlorine was used as a weapon. The poisonous gas was released onto the battlefield. The gas is heavier than air, so it sank into bunkers and killed anyone hiding there. Chlorine burns the skin and lungs, so soldiers wore thick clothes and had gas masks (even for their horses) to protect them against gas attacks.

Oxygen

Oxygen is one of the few non-metals found in its pure form in nature. Oxygen is a gas that makes up one-fifth of the air we breathe. It is also the most common element in Earth's rocks.

Oxygen is one of the most common elements on Earth. It makes up nearly two-thirds of the weight of your body. Oxygen is essential for life—we would die if we could not breathe it in. Our body uses oxygen to react with food to produce the energy that keeps us alive. The same kind of reaction causes burning, or combustion. There can be no fire or flames without oxygen.

Most of the pure oxygen in Earth's atmosphere is produced by plants. Plants produce oxygen as they use sunlight to produce sugar—a process called photosynthesis.

In its usual form, oxygen is an odorless, colorless, tasteless gas made up of molecules with two oxygen atoms bonded together. A more unusual form, called ozone, is found high in the atmosphere. The ozone layer protects us from dangerous rays in sunlight. An ozone molecule is made of three oxygen atoms bonded together.

When a substance such as wood or coal burns, it is reacting with oxygen in the air.

In large amounts, oxygen can kill bacteria, which makes it useful for cleaning water. Oxygen also reacts with nearly every other element. It reacts with carbon to make carbon dioxide gas. It oxidizes iron into rust, and burns with hydrogen to make water.

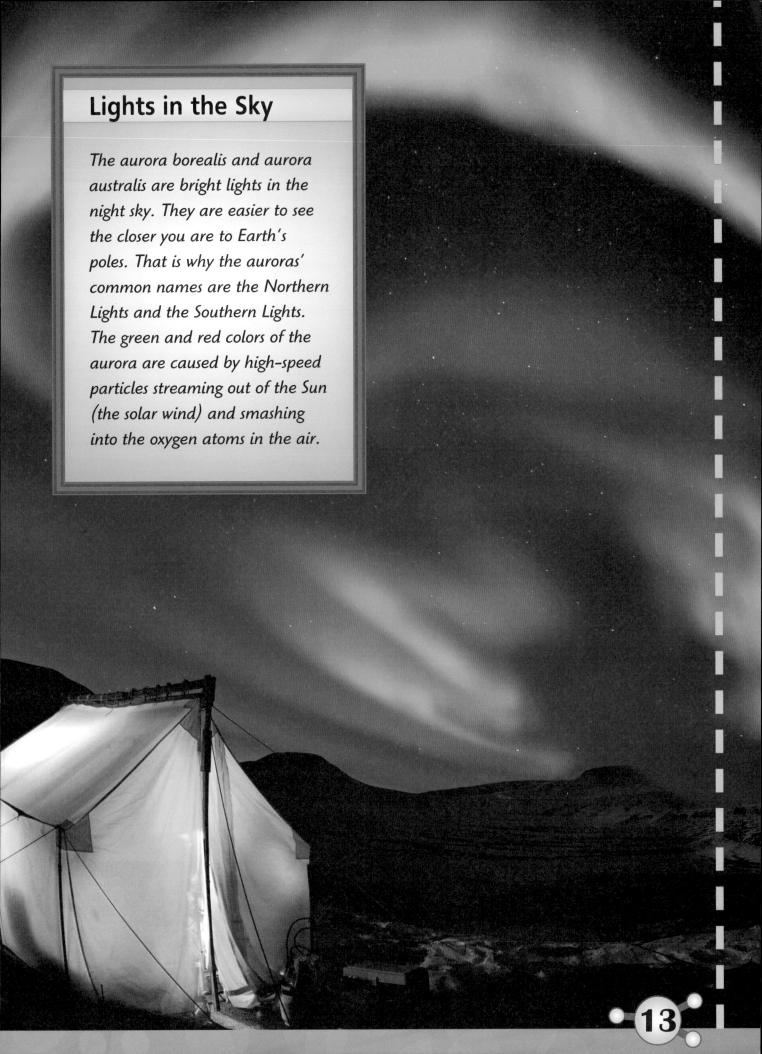

Lights in the Sky

The aurora borealis and aurora australis are bright lights in the night sky. They are easier to see the closer you are to Earth's poles. That is why the auroras' common names are the Northern Lights and the Southern Lights. The green and red colors of the aurora are caused by high-speed particles streaming out of the Sun (the solar wind) and smashing into the oxygen atoms in the air.

Sulfur

Sulfur is one of the pure solid non-metals. It forms yellow crystals around volcanoes and often has the odor, or smell, of rotten eggs.

Sulfur is in many other substances that have bad odors, including the smell of a skunk, rotting food, or burning hair. These odors come from natural products, and all life needs at least a little sulfur.

There are even animals in the deep ocean that could not survive without sulfur leaking out from volcanoes under the seabed. The sulfur compounds in the water are eaten by types of bacteria, then deep-sea worms and crabs eat the bacteria. On land, plants also need quite a bit of sulfur, so it is used in fertilizer (page 17).

However, like oxygen, large amounts of sulfur can kill. This makes it a good fungicide and insecticide.

Chunks of pure sulfur are dug up by miners working in volcanoes.

Sulfur-rich sprays are used to kill bugs living in buildings and remove pests that might damage crops growing in fields. Sulfur compounds are also added to foods. These substances prevent bacteria from making food rot but are still safe for us to eat.

Sulfur is a waste material from the process of purifying natural gas and petroleum. This is the source of most sulfur today. However, pure sulfur is also dug up in mines. Some people collect sulfur because its crystals have bright colors and interesting shapes. Melted sulfur is a deep red, which may be why it is also called brimstone. Pyrite, also known as fool's gold, contains sulfur.

Sulfur Balls

The first electricity generators were called sulfur balls. They were invented by German Otto von Guericke in the 1650s. The generator used a spinning ball of sulfur to create sparks of electricity. The ball also attracted feathers and similar light objects. (Rubbing a balloon does the same thing.) The sulfur ball was the first of many "friction machines" used to investigate electricity before the invention of the battery about 150 years later.

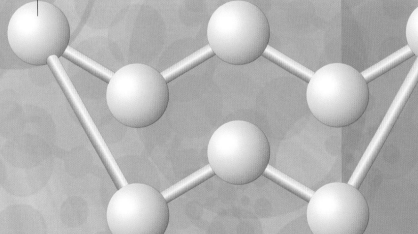

Sulfur atom

Pure sulfur forms a complicated structure of eight atoms that looks like a boat or crown.

Nitrogen

More than three-quarters of Earth's atmosphere is the non-metal gas nitrogen. This gas has no color or odor, and does not react easily with most other elements.

Nitrogen compounds called nitrates are found in fertilizers, which help plants grow.

Nitrogen is the most common gas in the air. However, nitrogen is not a very reactive element, so it does not do much. Even so, nitrogen compounds are essential for life. For example, nitrogen is found in proteins, which are the chemicals in muscles, skin, the blood, and many other body parts.

All animals get their nitrogen compounds from their food—other animals or plants. Plants get them from the soil. If the soil does not have many nitrogen compounds in it, the plants will not grow.

Bags of salad are filled with nitrogen. The gas prevents germs on the leaves from making them rot.

Farmers have always added nitrogen-rich material to fields to help plants grow. In the old days, this was compost (rotted plants) or muck (animal waste).

However, 100 years ago, **chemists** figured out how to take nitrogen from the air and turn it into fertilizers—chemicals that help plants grow. About one-third of Earth's population eats food grown in this way. Fertilizers are made by the Haber process, which reacts nitrogen and hydrogen together to make a compound called ammonia. Ammonia can then be made into useful chemicals such as fertilizers. Ammonia is also used to make cleaners, and explosives such as dynamite and TNT. The N in TNT stands for nitrogen.

Liquid Nitrogen

At room temperature, nitrogen is a gas. Nitrogen remains a gas until it is cooled to −320°F (−196°C), then it becomes liquid. Because liquid nitrogen is so very cold, it is used to flash freeze things and make them solid very quickly (see below). Doctors also use liquid nitrogen to freeze warts and moles so they can be cut off without causing bleeding. Liquid nitrogen is also used to cool supercomputers, which run so fast that they create a lot of heat. Liquid nitrogen is dangerous. It can cause burns on the skin.

Phosphorus

Phosphorus is a highly reactive element that glows in the dark. Phosphorus is found in our bodies, and is essential to all life. It is the first element that we can link to a discoverer.

Alchemists were wizard-like researchers who lived many centuries ago. They are known for trying to make gold out of other substances. One method they tried was to make gold from substances that had a similar color. They noticed a similarity between the colors of gold and **urine**, for example. About 350 years ago, German alchemist Hennig Brand tried to make gold by boiling urine. Instead of gold, Brand purified some phosphorus. The phosphorus glowed slightly, so Brand named it after a star. Hennig Brand is also the first person known to have discovered a new element.

Phosphorus is found in urine because it is used in many processes in the body. Phosphorus makes bones and teeth hard, and it is an important part of DNA. DNA is a complicated chemical that carries the instructions for making a living body.

Allotropes

Pure phosphorus is found in two forms, or allotropes—red phosphorus and white phosphorus. Both allotropes are poisonous non-metals that burn easily. White phosphorus is a waxy solid that glows in the dark. It catches fire as soon as it meets the air, producing thick smoke. Red phosphorus forms when white phosphorus is exposed to sunlight. It is less reactive than the white kind, and requires a high temperature to catch fire. Red phosphorus is used in matches.

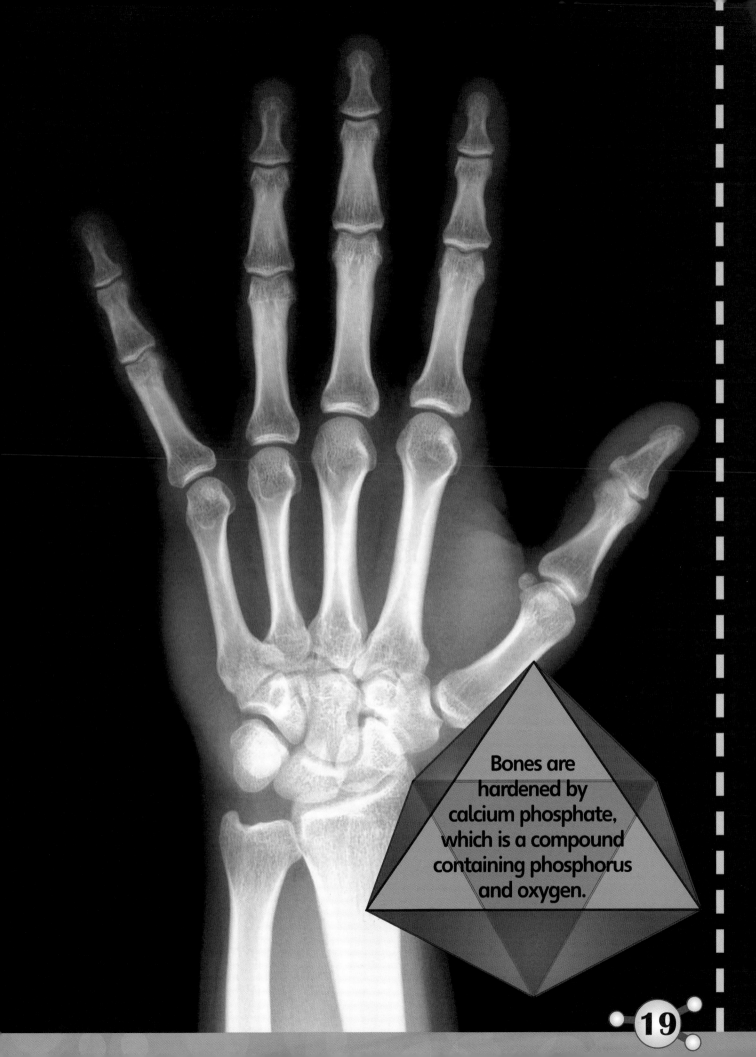

Bones are hardened by calcium phosphate, which is a compound containing phosphorus and oxygen.

Carbon

Carbon is an element found in all living things on Earth. Carbon is the element that is required for life. Experts say that our planet has "carbon-based life-forms."

A diamond is made from pure carbon.

Carbon is a very significant non-metal. In nature, it exists in four pure forms, or allotropes: diamond, graphite, charcoal (or soot), and buckyballs (also known as fullerenes). All forms of carbon are solids but they are all different. Diamond is the hardest natural substance there is, but graphite is slippery and rubs off on paper.

In Earth's atmosphere, carbon is found as carbon dioxide. This gas is breathed out by animals and is also produced when carbon-based fuels burn. The amount of carbon on Earth does not change, but the carbon moves through cycles. It is taken from the air by plants and converted into sugar. Animals eat the plants and breathe out carbon dioxide after burning the sugar as fuel to power their bodies.

In another carbon cycle, plants and other life forms that took in carbon dioxide get buried underground and decay into oil and coal over millions of years. These fuels are then dug up and burned by humans, and the carbon dioxide is released back into the atmosphere.

The carbon atom has four electrons available to bond with other atoms. There are 10 million compounds that we know contain carbon. They are in the smoke that makes smog, and in the black soot from flames. Plastic contains carbon bonded with hydrogen. Methane, propane, and other fuels are made of carbon and hydrogen.

When carbon is added to iron, it makes super-strong steel. Graphite is in pencil lead and lightweight sports equipment. Even chalk and limestone contain carbon.

Pencil lead is made from graphite, which is a pure form of carbon. It leaves a thin layer of carbon on the paper.

Carbon Nanotubes

Diamond is made from carbon atoms arranged in pyramids. In graphite, the atoms are arranged in hexagons.

Scientists roll a sheet of graphite that is one single atom thick into tubes. They are called nanotubes (see above). (Nano means "billionth.") These nanotubes are much too small to see. A nanotube long enough to go to the Moon would roll up into a ball the size of a poppy seed. Even though the nanotubes are thin, they are very strong. In the future, we might use nanotubes to make buildings and vehicles that are super strong and super light.

Hydrogen

Hydrogen has the smallest and simplest atom, and is the lightest of all elements. Hydrogen gas has no color, no taste, and no smell, but it is highly flammable.

Because it reacts so easily with other elements, pure hydrogen does not exist in nature. Hydrogen bonds easily with almost all other elements to form substances. The most common substance hydrogen bonds with is water.

Hydrogen is an unusual non-metal. It has the smallest atom, with just one proton at the center and circled by just one electron. All the other elements that have one outer electron are classed as metals. But hydrogen is a non-metal gas. The atom's simple electron shell has room for just two electrons. So, hydrogen's outer shell is half full. The shell can lose one electron in reactions but it can also gain one.

So hydrogen can form a positive ion, like sodium or another metal, but it can also share electrons with other atoms. This is how it forms a water molecule (see box on page 23).

In chemistry, hydrogen is a very important element. The reacting power of an acid or alkali is measured as pH, which is a way of counting how many hydrogen ions they have. Acids have high numbers of hydrogen ions, and alkalies have low numbers.

All acids, such as the one that gives a lemon its sour taste, contain hydrogen.

Water

Two-thirds of Earth is covered by water. Chemists call water H_2O. That means that each molecule of water consists of two hydrogen atoms and one oxygen atom. A bucket of water is two-thirds hydrogen. Earth is the only place in the solar system where water is liquid. Everywhere else, it is solid ice or water vapor. Astronomers think that much of Earth's oceans came from icy comets that crashed into the planet.

Oil and Fuel

Hydrocarbons are naturally occurring substances made only from hydrogen and carbon. Hydrocarbons are found in petroleum, such as crude oil and coal. Many are used as fuels. Others are used to make useful substances such as plastics and painkillers.

Hydrogen and carbon can form nearly endless chains of atoms. Because they can bond in many patterns, there are many thousands of hydrocarbons. The carbons form the spine of the molecule. These atoms can bond to four atoms in all. The hydrogen atoms can only bond to one other at the same time, so they stick out of the central carbon atoms.

Most natural hydrocarbons are found in petroleum—a thick oil that comes from deep underground. (The word *petroleum* means "rock oil.") These hydrocarbons are used to make many varied materials, including plastics, medicines, and fuels. Hydrocarbons come in all states of matter. Methane and propane fuels are gases, and benzene, gasoline, and kerosene are liquids. Solid hydrocarbons are known as waxes and tars. Polyethylene is a solid plastic used in bottles and bags. It is made by linking millions of molecules of a gas compound called ethylene.

Crude oil is a mixture of hundreds of compounds. They are separated in oil refineries.

Hydrocarbons are said to be hydrophobic—they will not mix with water. This is why cooking oil or motor oil floats on top of water when the two are poured into a glass. Hydrocarbon waxes are a traditional covering for waterproofing fabrics.

Most hydrocarbons are hazardous to human health. Benzene is very dangerous and must be handled with care. It causes **cancers** such as leukemia. There are very tiny amounts of benzene in the environment leaking from factories and refineries. Food producers must test their items for benzene and more dangerous hydrocarbons.

Plastic is made from small hydrocarbon molecules that have been chained together.

Petrochemical Count

Make a list of the petrochemicals in your home. How many can you identify? Here are a few suggestions below. We are surrounded by objects made of the hydrocarbons from crude oil, including:

plastic
makeup
aerosol sprays
baby oil
paint
nylon and other materials
painkillers
computer screens (liquid crystals)
superglue

Noble Gases

The noble gases form what is often called Group 8 in the periodic table. The six noble gases are helium, neon, argon, krypton, xenon, and the radioactive radon. They are described as noble because they do not interact with other elements.

All of the noble elements exist as gases at room temperature. Under normal room conditions, the noble gases are odorless, colorless, and will not burn. The noble gases do not really form any compounds because the outer electron shells of their atoms are completely full. There is no space for any more electrons, so the elements do not need to bond with other atoms. This makes the noble gases inert, which means inactive. Noble gases are in the air all around us, and in use all around us, too. Helium is used in balloons, light bulbs, and air tanks for deep-sea diving. At very high pressure, deep underwater, too much oxygen can be deadly.

Argon gas is used by welders. It prevents the hot metals from reacting with oxygen.

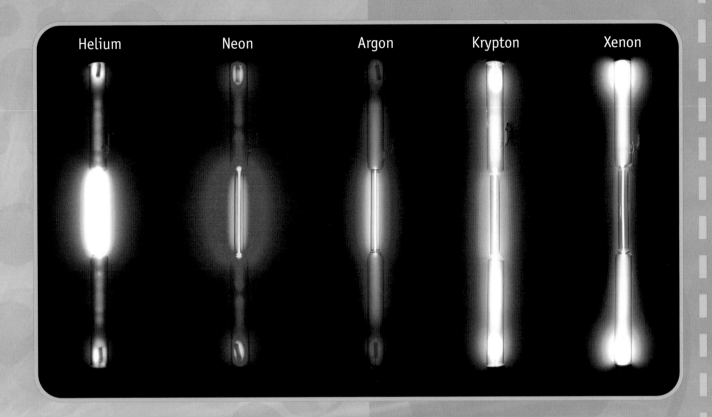

| Helium | Neon | Argon | Krypton | Xenon |

Helium is a very light gas—only hydrogen gas is lighter. However, unlike hydrogen airships, helium airships cannot explode.

Adding helium to the air mixture that divers breathe makes it safer for them to use.

Noble gases have been used to make colored lights for many years. They are less common now but so-called neon lights once lit up the world's city centers. The gases, especially krypton and argon, are still used to make laser lights. Laser lights are used in light shows and to make pictures of the inside of the body using a medical CT (CAT) scan.

Neon Lights

Each noble gas glows when it produces energy. This makes noble gases useful for making lights. For example, a neon light is made by coating the inside of a glass tube with a thin layer of fluorescent, or bright and glowing, powder then filling the tube with neon gas. When a powerful electric current is run through the gas, the energy jumps from one neon atom to the next. This makes them produce light, which creates the glow. The term "neon light" is sometimes used to mean any gas-discharge light. Neon produces a bright red light. The other noble gases are used to produce different colors (see above). The glass tubes used for neon lights can be heated and bent into words and shapes.

Discovery of Helium

In 1868, astronomers saw the color of an unknown gas in the light from the Sun. It became easier to see when a solar eclipse cut out the glare (above). English chemist Norman Lockyer named the substance helium, from the Greek word helios, meaning "Sun." About 14 years later, an Italian physicist named Luigi Palmieri detected helium in the lava from a volcano. In 1895, the Scottish chemist Sir William Ramsay was able to collect a sample of helium gas coming out of crystals from Norway. Each researcher identified the gas from its distinctive color that matched the one seen all those years before in sunlight.

High-temperature welding equipment melts metals so they can be joined together. Argon is used to shield the hot metal from reactive oxygen in the air. Liquid neon is used for deep freezing, while xenon is used as anesthetic (painkiller) during surgery. Radon is also used by doctors. The radioactivity the gas gives off can be targeted to kill cancers inside bodies.

Small amounts of radon gas are given off by rocks such as granite.

Radon Gas

Radon is a colorless and odorless noble gas. However, radon is radioactive and that makes it a health hazard. Radon comes out of rocks, such as granite, shale, and limestone. The gas is produced when other elements in the rock break down into it. Radon gas comes out of gravel and rocks and builds up in the basements of houses. Radon atoms also break apart, so the amount of the gas constantly goes higher and lower. Radon is dangerous and can cause lung cancer. People who live in radon areas use fans to blow away the gas. Radon can also be helpful. For example, radon is used in creating nuclear power.

Glossary

acid A substance that gives out positive hydrogen atoms in water; a substance with a low pH value; any substance that neutralizes an alkaline (base) substance

allotropes Forms of a pure element that are physically different from each other

atom The smallest unit of an element

cancer A disease that makes the body grow damaging lumps; cancer can be caused by radioactive radiation

charge The property of ions and some subatomic particles; objects with an overall negative charge attract objects with a positive charge. Objects with the same charge push each other away.

chemist A scientist who studies the elements and figures out how substances are formed from combinations of atoms

compound A substance made up of two or more elements that have combined during a chemical reaction

conduct To transmit energy such as heat or electricity

electron A tiny negatively charged particle that is found in atoms

electron shell One of the layers in which electrons are arranged around the outside of an atom

element A simple natural substance that cannot be simplified into any other substances

gas The state of matter in which a substance is made up of small units that move independently of each other in all directions; steam is the gas form of water

insulators Materials that do not conduct heat or electricity easily

ion A charged particle that is formed when an atom loses or gains one or more electrons

liquid The state of matter in which a substance is made up of small units that are connected together but can flow around each other. Liquids have a fixed volume but no fixed shape.

metal An element that is a hard and shiny solid; metal elements have atoms with only a few outer electrons

metalloid Any of the elements that share a combination of properties of metals and non-metals

molecule A combination of atoms that are arranged in a certain way

neutron A subatomic particle with no charge

non-metal An element that is not a metal; non-metal atoms have many electrons in their outer shells

proton A subatomic particle with a positive charge

react To produce a chemical process in which the atoms in substances are rearranged, creating new compounds or splitting them into pure elements

solid The state of matter in which a substance is made up of small units that are all locked together. A solid has a fixed volume and fixed shape.

urine The scientific name for the liquid waste humans and other animals produce

Index

Web Finder

www.ptable.com/

www.eia.gov/kids/index.cfm

http://encyclopedia.kids.net.au/page/no/non-metal

www.chem4kids.com/files/atom_bonds.html